Explanation of Ibn Qayyim's Thirteen Conditions for an Accepted Dua

Shaykh Abdur Razzaaq al Badr

Copyright 2022

Table of Contents

Introduction

In the Name of Allaah, the Most Merciful, the Bestower of Mercy

All praise is due to Allaah, the Lord of all creation. May Allaah bestow His praise, manifest his virtue and exalt the status of the noblest of the Prophets and the Seal of the Messengers, our Prophet Muhammad and protect him, the message of Islam, his family and all his companions from any harm in this life or the next.

In fact, Allaah commanded His worshipers to make du'a and He promised them an answer in many verses of His Book (the Noble Quran). In several verses in His Book, Allaah commanded His slaves to supplicate to Him and promised them that He will respond. Allaah said:

"And your Lord said: Call on Me, I will answer your [call or invocation]. Verily, those who scorn My worship, they will surely enter Hell in humiliation!"[1] (1 Surah al-Ghafir: 60)

And He said:

"My Lord is verily the Hearer of all supplications."[2] (2 Surah Ibrahim: 39)

And Allaah said:

"And when My worshipers ask you (O Muhammad) about Me, then I am indeed near. I respond to the invocations of the supplicant when he supplicates to Me (without any mediator or intercessor). So let them obey Me and believe in Me, that they may be rightly guided."

And He said:

"Call upon your Lord with humility and in secret. Indeed, He does not love the aggressors. And do not cause mischief on the earth after it has been set in order, and call upon Him with fear and hope; verily, Allaah's mercy is close to those who do good deeds."[2]

And the verses (in the Quran) with this meaning are abundant. Allaah has indeed encouraged His worshipers to make du'a and He has urged them to do so, although He is free of needing them (He is not in any need of His creation) and their du'a (their supplications and their acts of worship). Just as He (the Most High) said in Hadeeth Qudsee [3]:

"O My worshippers (slaves)! You can never harm Me or bring Me any benefit. O My worshippers! If the first of you and the last of you, the human of you and the jinn of you, were like the heart of the most pious man among you, it would not add anything to My dominion. O My worshippers! If the first of you and the last of you, the human of you and the jinn of you, were as evil as the heart of the most evil man, it would not detract from My dominion. O My worshippers! If the first of you and the last of you, the human of you and the jinn of you, were to stand on a single plain and pray to Me, and I were to give everyone what they asked for, it would not diminish what is with Me, except what a needle decreases from the ocean when it is dipped into it…"[4]

So, Allaah is not benefited by the supplication of the supplicant nor the humility of the one who humbles himself. However, despite all this, Allaah loves that His slave ask Him.

And along with that, He loves that His worshipers pray to Him (and ask from Him). Rather, the greater the worshiper's concern for making du'a, the greater his share and portion of the love that Allaah has for him. Every time the concern for supplication is magnified by the slave, the portion of the love of Allaah is magnified for him. So much so that the Prophet (peace and blessings of Allaah be upon him) said:

"There is nothing more honorable (noble) to Allaah Most High than the du'a (supplication)." [5] And he (peace and blessings of Allaah be upon him) said:

"Whoever does not ask Allaah, then He becomes angry with him."[6]

[A poet said:]

Allaah gets angry if you abandon asking (supplicating to) Him,
while the children of Adam get angry when they are asked.

So, the Lord of all creation loves those who ask, and He promised them that He would answer their du'a, and that He would make their hopes come true, and that He would give them what they ask for (fulfill their request); as long as they fulfill the statutory conditions when making their du'a and any preventative factors are removed. The text from the Book of Allaah and the Sunnah of the Messenger of Allaah (peace and blessings of Allaah be upon him) shows that the supplication described as not being rejected has criteria. In fact, many texts in the Book of Allaah and the Sunnah of the Messenger of Allaah (peace and blessings of Allaah be upon him) show that the accepted du'a has rules that are necessary for the one making the du'a to be diligent in following them when making his du'a. Likewise, there are preventive factors that he must take care of so that his du'a is not rejected. Its explanations have come in the Book of Allaah and the Sunnah of His Prophet (peace and blessings of Allaah be upon him). The scholars have called them: the conditions and etiquettes of supplicating. And they are extremely important. It is befitting for the one supplicating while supplicating to be intent on carrying out the etiquettes of supplicating so that his supplication is answered. And to be aware of the affairs that prevent it from being accepted so his supplication won't be rejected.

And this affair is extensive. However, I've found an excellent concise summary of it by the Imam Ibn al-Qayyim in a few lines. He gathered the most important affairs for the supplicant to give concern to.

Al-'Allamah, al-Imam Ibn al-Qayyim (Allaah have mercy on him) compiled an amazing summary containing a huge amount of good in which he (Allaah have mercy on him) specified the most important of what is appropriate for those making du'a to concern themselves about when they call upon Allaah (the Most High). Then he concluded his speech after enumerating these rules for making du'a with the statement: "This du'a (the supplication made with all these rules), indeed, it is rare that it would be rejected."[7]

Though his rules consists of a few line. However it contains tremendous good and benefits in regards to what the one supplicating to Allaah (the Most High) should give concern to so that his supplication is answered and not rejected.

Therefore, it is from good advice and a desire to spread his speech along with a commentary on it that will clarify his intentions and magnify the benefits. At the beginning, I will simply list his full speech (and then I will comment on each sentence, one by one). I will mention the source and evidence of the each statement either from the Book of Allaah or from the Sunnah of His Messenger (peace and blessings of Allaah be upon him).

Al-Imam Ibn al-Qayyim (Allaah have mercy on him) said,[8]

"If a prayer is combined with (the he enumerates the points one by one):

❖ the presence of the heart and its awareness of the goal,

❖ and coinciding with the six prescribed times of acceptance - and they are: the last third of the night, at the time of the adhan, between the adhan and the iqamah, at the end of the prescribed prayers, from the time the imam ascends the minbar on the day of Jumu'ah until the salah is finished and the last hour (on Jumu'ah) after 'Asr,

❖ and coinciding with submission in heart and repentance before the Lord, feeling insignificant, imploring and weak,

❖ and whoever makes du'a faces the qiblah,

❖ and he is in a state of purity,

❖ and he raises his hands to Allaah,

❖ and he begins with praises and glorifications of Allaah,

❖ then he sends salutations to Muhammad (peace and blessings of Allaah be upon him), His worshiper and His messenger by asking Allaah to grant him praise, manifest his virtue and raise his status,

❖ then he declares, before anything else, his need for repentance and forgiveness,

❖ then he persistently declares his dire need of repentance and flatters Him,

❖ and he calls upon Him with longing and reverence,

❖ and seeks intercession with His Names, His Attributes and His Oneness,

❖ and he precedes his du'a with charity,

"This (such a) du'a, indeed, it is rare that it would be rejected."

❖ Especially if it matches with the prayers that the Prophet (peace and blessings of Allaah be upon him) has informed us are most likely to be answered and they contain Allaah's Greatest Name.[9]

The First Condition

The presence of the heart and its awareness of the goal.

The first condition is that the Muslim makes du'a with a present heart. Meaning that he supplicates while his heart is present. The presence of the heart is to turn to Allaah so that his du'a does not merely move his tongue while his heart is heedless. Instead, he moves his tongue with du'a while having presence of heart. About this the Prophet (peace and blessings of Allaah be upon him) said in an authentic Hadeeth:

"Make du'a (supplicate) to Allaah while you are sure (certain) of being answered, and know that Allaah does not answer the du'a from the heart of the heedless, the distracted (inattentive)."[10]

From the signs of the lack of presence of the heart when making du'a is an abundance of preoccupation and movements at the time of du'a. So you find that his tongue moves with the du'a and his hands play with the ground or with his clothes or anything other than that; or you find him turning his gaze to the right and left at the time of his du'a. All this is because the heart is not present at the time of asking Allaah (the Most High).

Because of this, when 'Umar ibn 'Abdul-Azeez (Allaah haver mercy on him) saw a man making du'a and in his hand there were pebbles and he was playing with them, he said to him:

"If only you had thrown down the pebbles and made yourself sincere to Allaah in du'a."[11]

And there has come in our time a new pebble of a different type, which is in the hands of people most of the time. The hearts are taken up in this great lump of amusement, and play more than their hands are. So he is unable to make du'a well or supplicate and ask. To these it is necessary that it be said to them: "If only you had switched off your phone and made yourself sincere to Allaah by asking."

So the first concern for the one who wants Allaah to answer his du'a is to turn his heart to Allaah when making du'a. And he should fight against himself to concentrate his heart and thoughts on his goal and his need and not occupy himself with anything but making du'a to his Lord (the Most High). The heart splits in many directions if it is neglected. Therefore, there is no doubt that one should strive to collect his heart and make it present at the time of du'a.

The Second Condition

Coinciding with the prescribed acceptance times (for the prayer).

Al-Imam Ibn al-Qayyim (Allaah have mercy on him) listed six places:

The first: the last third of the night. This time is counted from the most probable times of acceptance of du'a and the greatest of them in status. This is because of what is established in the two Saheehs of the Prophet (peace and blessings of Allaah be upon him) that he said:

"Our Lord descends every night to the sky of the dunya when there is a third of the night left, and He says: 'Who calls Me that I may answer him? Who asks Me that I may give him? Who seeks My forgiveness so that I may forgive him?'"[12] This hadith shows that this tremendous and blessed time is from the most likely times of acceptance. Therefore, it is appropriate for every Muslim to strive to benefit from this good and that he strive with complete aspiration that he does not miss a night except that he invokes Allaah at this blessed time.

The second: at the time of the adhan, which means immediately after the adhan. This is a great time to pursue making du'a.

This is a different time than the third place, which is next: between adhan and iqamah. In fact, the texts have shown that whoever listens to the adhan repeats after the mu'adhdhin and then immediately makes du'a after it, then his du'a will be accepted.

This is because of what 'Abdullah ibn 'Amr (Allaah be pleased with him) narrated: that a man said to the Prophet (peace and blessings of Allaah be upon him), "O Messenger of Allaah! Indeed, the mu'adhdhin are above us." – i.e., they have advanced us in virtue. So the Prophet (peace and blessings of Allaah be upon him) said:

"Say as they say, and when you are finished, ask and you will be given."[13] This hadith shows the connection between the virtue of this du'a and listening to the adhan and answering the mu'adhdhin.

Thus, it is appropriate for the Muslim to listen to the adhan and repeat its words after the mu'adhdhin and follow it with what has come in the Sunnah, to send salah and salam upon the Prophet (peace and blessings of Allaah be upon him) and ask Allaah to give the Prophet (peace and blessings of Allaah be upon him) the highest place in Paradise and to give him excellence. It is appropriate for him not to stop there but to follow it with a du'a for what he desires because this is a great time to seek an answer.

The third: between adhan and iqamah. A number of texts have appeared on the virtue of du'a between adhan and iqamah in all circumstances. From them is the statement of the Prophet (peace and blessings of Allaah be upon him):

"The du'a between adhan and iqamah is not rejected."[14] And the Prophet (peace and blessings of Allaah be upon him) said:

"When salah is called, the gates of heaven are opened and the du'a is accepted."[15] It is therefore appropriate for the believer that he is abundant in making du'a for himself at this time and seeking goodness from the Lord of all creation.

The fourth: at the end of the prescribed prayers, which means before tasleem, because this time is virtuous and it is believed that the du'a of the one who prays during it is accepted. This is because it has collected a number of reasons for the acceptance of du'a in it: the Muslim is in a state of purity, he faces the qiblah, he exalts Allaah and magnifies Him and recites His Speech. He then bows and prostrates in submission and humility before Allaah, the Lord of all creation.

So when he sits for tashahhud after these tremendous actions, he begins by saying words that imply peace, sovereignty and eternity, which belong to Allaah and exalt His Greatness, saying: 'At- Tahiayatu lillahi was-salawatu wat-tayyibatu ...' Then he bears witness to the Tawheed of Allaah, and then he sends salah to the Prophet (peace and blessings of Allaah be upon him) with the most complete form of sending salah which is Salah al-Ibraheemiyyah. So all that has gone before from the high positions of worship makes this time one of the most important times for Allaah to accept the du'a of those who ask when they pray. Regarding this, there is the hadith of Ibn Mas'ud (Allaah be pleased with him) where the Prophet (peace and blessings of Allaah be upon him) taught tashahhud and at the end of it he said:

"Then he should select the du'a that is most pleasing to him and make du'a (with it)."[16]

The fifth: from the time the imam mounts the minbar on the day of Jumu'ah until the salah is completed. This is because of what is authentically reported from the Prophet (peace and blessings of Allaah be upon him) that he said:

"Indeed, on Jumu'ah there is an hour no Muslim happens to stand and pray during it, asking Allaah for good, except that He gives him what he asked for." And with his hand he illustrated the shortness of that time.[17] A group of scholars have said that this hour is from the time the Imam mounts the minbar until he finishes Salat-ul-Jumu'ah. This is because of what Imam Muslim reported in his Saheeh from Abu Musa al -Ash'aree (Allaah be pleased with him):

"It is between the time when the imam sits until he finishes salah."[18] This hadith is narrated from Abu Musa in a manner elevated to the Prophet (peace and blessings of Allaah be upon him). It is also narrated in a manner that stops at Abu Musa and is considered to be from his speech. It is because of this that a number of scholars preferred the view that the hour of acceptance is at this point.

As a result, it is appropriate that the Muslim is mindful of saying 'Ameen' to the khateeb's du'a, and that he engages in abundant du'a during Salat-ul-Jumu'ah. This is because, as it is before, the virtue of this hour extends until the salah ends. [He should make du'a] especially during prostration because it has been authentically narrated from the Prophet (peace and blessings of Allaah be upon him) that he said:

"The closest a worshiper is to his Lord is when he is prostrating. So be abundant in making du'a."[19]

Similarly, he should strive to make du'a after tashahhud before the Imam gives salam, because it is from the places where the du'a was accepted - as it has preceded.

The sixth: the last hour after 'Asr, meaning the last hour after 'Asr until the sun sets on the day of Jumu'ah. Indeed, it has been authentically reported from the Prophet (peace and blessings of Allaah be upon him) that he said:

"The day of Jumu'ah is twelve hours. No Muslim asks Allaah for anything except that Allaah gives it to him. So stick to the last hour after 'Asr.'[20] Because of this al-'Allamah Ibn al-Qayyim (Allaah have mercy on him) mentioned in his book Zad-ul-Ma'ad that the strongest and most likely opinion to define the virtuous hour on the day of Jumu'ah when the du'a is not rejected is "the two previous statements. The first: when the imam climbs the minbar until the salah is finished. And the second: the last hour after 'Asr until the sun sets on the day of Jumu'ah."[21]

Thus it behooves the worshiper who desires good for himself not to miss these two virtuous times. On the contrary, he strives during both of them to make du'a and asking (Allaah), singling out these two times with increased concern, so that he may obtain the good that he seeks and hopes for from the Lord of all creation.

The Third Condition

Submission of the heart and repentance before the Lord, with humility and submission

This matter, which Imam Ibn al-Qayyim (Allaah have mercy on him) mentioned, is of utmost importance in the matter of du'a as well as other acts of worship. From the completion of the worship is that the worshiper supplicates and is meek before his Creator and Master (the Most High) especially when he makes du'a and requests, as Allaah Most High said:

"Call upon your Lord with submission and humility. Indeed, He does not love the aggressors."[22]

At-Tabaree said in his Tafseer: "Tazarruan" (in the above verse) means to be meek and submissive in obedience to Him, and "Wakhufyatan" means the humbleness of their hearts."[23]

It is appropriate that submission and repentance take over the state of the one making du'a when he asks his Lord, and that he supplicates to Him in a lowered voice in humility and with manners. Regarding this, when the Prophet (peace and blessings of Allaah be upon him) heard some of the Sahabah (Allaah be pleased with them) raising their voices in dhikr and du'a, he said to them:

"O people! Be merciful to yourselves. In reality, you are not calling on a deaf or an absent one. Indeed, you are calling on the One who hears and is near, and He is with you."[24]

Al -Hafidh Ibn Hajar (Allaah have mercy on him) said: "This hadith contains a dislike to raise the voice in du'a and dhikr. This is what the generality of the Salaf were on from the Sahabah and the Ta'bi'een."[25]

Al -Hafidh An-Nawawee (Allaah have mercy on him) made a chapter for this hadith entitled: "The recommendation to lower the voice in dhikr except for the times when the legislation comes to raise it."

The Fourth Condition

Facing the qiblah at the time of du'a

Facing the qiblah is considered from the exalted manners of du'a, which shows the respect that the one making du'a has for the affair of du'a and his concern for it.

Regarding this, it has been authentically narrated from the Prophet (peace and blessings of Allaah be upon him) in a number of situations that he would face the qiblah and make du'a, just as it happened in the Battle of Badr when he (peace and blessings of Allaah be upon him) saw the abundant amount of polytheists compared to the amount of Muslims. So the Prophet of Allaah (peace and blessings of Allaah be upon him) faced the qiblah and then he stretched out his hands.[27]

This is because facing the qiblah for the one making du'a is one of the reasons it is hoped that his du'a will be accepted. It is not from the requirements of du'a, but rather it is from the praiseworthy manners.

The Fifth Condition

Purification when making du'a

Purification is also from the manners of du'a. There is no doubt that if the person making du'a is in a state of purification, then it is better and more complete for his du'a and his secret counsel with Allaah (the Most High) because the state of being in wudu is without exception better than the state of being in the state of impurity.

On the authority of al-Muhajir ibn Qunfudh (Allaah be pleased with him) who said that he gave salaams to the Prophet (peace and blessings of Allaah be upon him) and he was performing wudu , so he (peace and blessings of Allaah be upon him) did not answer him until he completed wudu. Then he answered and said:

"Nothing prevented me from answering you except that I do not like to mention Allaah except while I was in the state of purification."[28]

The Sixth Condition

Raising the hands when making du'a

Salman al-Farisee (Allaah be pleased with him) narrated that the Prophet (peace and blessings of Allaah be upon him) said:

"Indeed, your Lord is Shy, Ever Generous. He is Shy to allow a worshiper's hands to return empty after he raised them up to Him."[29]

Allaah (the Most High), the One who is free from all needs, is Shy to return the hands of his worshipers empty if they raise them to him; meaning without anything in them. This is because the state of raising the hands to the sky - turning the palms to the sky or to the face - is considered a posture of need, humility and repentance, and it shows neediness and distress, therefore it is a reason for the acceptance of du'a with Allaah.

The ahadeeth where the Prophet (peace and blessings of Allaah be upon him) raised his hands and made du'a are many. In fact, he (peace and blessings of Allaah be upon him) used to exaggerate in raising his hands in extremely difficult times, more than in other times, as was said earlier about the battle of Badr, when he (peace and blessings of Allaah be upon him) saw the abundant number of polytheists compared to the number of Muslims. The Prophet (peace and blessings of Allaah be upon him) faced the qiblah and then he stretched out his hands in du'a to his Lord. 'Umar Ibn al -Khattab (Allaah be pleased with him) said:

"So he did not stop calling upon his Lord and stretched out his hands towards the qiblah until his upper garment fell from his shoulders."[30] Likewise at the time of the drought when he (peace and blessings of Allaah be upon him) made du'a on the minbar and asked for rain. Anas ibn Malik (Allaah be pleased with him) said:

"I saw the Messenger of Allaah (peace and blessings of Allaah be upon him) raise his hands in du'a until the whiteness of his armpits could be seen."[31]

The Seventh Condition

Beginning with the praises and glorification of Allaah and then asking Allaah to grant His Prophet Muhammad, manifest his virtue and raise his status before making du'a.

On the authority of Fudalah ibn 'Ubayd (Allaah be pleased with him) who said: "The Messenger of Allaah (peace and blessings of Allaah be upon him) heard a man making a du'a in his salah and he did not magnify Allaah, the Most High, and he did not send salah upon the Prophet (peace and blessings of Allaah be upon him), so the Prophet (peace and blessings of Allaah be upon him) said:

"This one has been hasty." Then he called that person and he said to him:

"When one of you prays, let him begin by glorifying his Lord and praising Him, and then let him send salah upon the Prophet (peace and blessings of Allaah be upon him), then he may ask for whatever he wants."[32]

It is more complete for the Muslim when he begins his du'a that he begins his du'a by praising Allaah and magnifying His greatness and praising Him. Then he combines it with sending salah and salam upon the Prophet (peace and blessings of Allaah be upon him) then he makes du'a after that to his Lord for what he likes.

With this we know the reason for the virtue of making du'a after hearing the adhan and its virtue after the last tashahhud - as it has preceded. Both these times are preceded by the praise and magnification of Allaah and the sending of salah and salam upon His Messenger Muhammad (peace and blessings of Allaah be upon him). So it is appropriate to make du'a at these two times of acceptance.[33]

The Eighth Condition

To repent and seek forgiveness before making du'a

Sins are certainly one of the preventive factors and influential barriers against acceptance of du'a. It has been authentically reported from the Prophet (peace and blessings of Allaah be upon him) that he mentioned:

"A man had traveled a long way. His hair was unkempt and he was covered in dust. He stretched out his hands towards the sky and said: 'O my Lord! O my Lord!' But his food was haram, his drink was haram, his clothes were haram, and he was nourished with haram. So how can his du'a be accepted?"[34]

So this man in his du'a had fulfilled a number of reasons for acceptance. He called upon his Lord as he traveled, and he raised his hands to the sky. But he did not abstain from haram; so, his clothes were haram, his food and his drink were from haram. It was thus a barrier and an obstacle to the acceptance of his du'a.

One of the Salaf said:

"Do not take the answer to your du'a to be slow, for it is possible that you have blocked its path with sins."[35]

Regarding this, the Prophet (peace and blessings of Allaah be upon him) used to seek forgiveness from

Allaah and repent to Him a hundred times a day. And he used to encourage his ummah to do so as well. He said:

"O people! Repent to Allaah, for verily I repent to Him a hundred times a day."[36] It is fitting for the believer who desires good for himself that he be abundant in asking for forgiveness and repenting along with recognizing and acknowledging his sins and having remorse for them, and having a strong conviction not to return to committing them. This is especially true when he makes du'a to his Lord (the Most High) as it is a reason for Allaah to pardon him and it is more conducive to the acceptance of his du'a and that he gets what he asked for.

The Ninth Condition

Being persistent in making du'a and not being impatient in wanting an answer

Abu Hurairah (Allaah be pleased with him) narrated that the Prophet (peace and blessings of Allaah be upon him) said:

"The supplication of one of you is answered as long as he is not impatient and says: I supplicated to my Lord, but I was not answered."39 (Reported by al-Bukharee in his Saheeh, no. 6240, and by Muslim in his Saheeh, no. 2735, and the wording is his.)

From the immense manners of du'a, it is being earnest when asking and repeating the du'a, and being consistent in asking along with utilizing the virtuous times (of asking). He who consistently knocks on the door for his there is hope that it will be opened to him.

Whoever considers the du'a of the people of understanding mentioned at the end of Surah Ali 'Imran, [will note] how they kept repeating the statement 'Our Lord' five times in their du'a, then it came at the end of it His statement:

"So their Lord answered (their prayer)."

Surah Ali 'Imran: 195

It is befitting for the worshiper not to rush the answer. Rushing the answer is from one of the many harms which prevents the effects of the du'a from falling into place. The one who is impatient, when he sees the answer coming slowly, gets tired and is likely to stop making du'a. So his condition will be like the condition of a person who sows a seed or plants a plant and he began to maintain it and water it and when he found its maturity and it took a long time to bear fruit, he gave it up, and he forgot about it. He did not get what he wanted from it.[37]

Al-Imam Ibn Al-Qayyim has drawn attention to this subtle benefit when he said, "he continually expresses his dire need for repentance and flatters him (to achieve his need)."[38] The word (here translated as) 'flatters' means to be kind and try to win someone's favor when asking. So he (Allaah have mercy on him) instructed that this persistence in making du'a should be done with kindness, with manners and with showing one's poverty, one's need for Allaah, the Lord of all creation.

The Tenth Condition

Combining both hope and fear in his du'a

Combining both hope and fear is a matter of utmost importance in the subject of du'a and in other acts of worship. It is appropriate for the believer to go back and forth between hope and fear in his acts of worship. Regarding this, when Allaah mentioned the stories of the Prophets (peace be upon them) in Surah al-Anbiya and how He rescued them from the difficulties and trials, He ended with His statement:

> "Verily, they used to hasten to do good deeds, and they used to call upon Us with hope and fear, and they used to humble themselves before Us."[39]

So they gathered in their du'a between 'raghbah' and 'rahbah'. 'Raghbah' is hoping for what is with Allaah, so the one who makes the du'a asks his Lord while he is hopeful for His grace and His bounties, and 'rahbah' is fear from His wrath and from the pain from His punishment.

When Allaah mentioned the complete attributes of the believers, He said:

> "And those who give what they give with their hearts full of fear."[40]

They strive in worship to obtain the reward of the Lord of all creation, and along with that their hearts are afraid that their actions will not be accepted. So they gather between hope and fear in their worship. Just like that is what has come in the du'a of Khaleel-ur-Rahman (friend of ar-Rahman), Ibraheem (peace be upon him) when Allaah commanded him to build the Sacred House of Allaah. So, he (peace be upon him) made du'a:

"Our Lord accept from us. Verily, You are All-hearing All-Knowing."[41]

And he is from those Messengers who are described as having strong will and determination, and Allaah took him as His Khaleel (friend) and he gave him the mission of performing one of the most noble acts, which was building the Sacred House of Allaah. After all that, he used to call upon Allaah, worried about Him accepting (that is not accepting) this action from Him. Regarding this, when Wuhayb ibn Ward (Allaah have mercy on him) recited this Ayah, he wept and said:

"O Khaleel-ur-Rahman! You built the foundation of the house of ar-Rahman and you were worried that it would not be accepted from you!"[42]

The Eleventh Condition

Seeking intercession by means of His Names, His Attributes and His Oneness

Seeking a means of nearness to Allaah with His Names and His Attributes is considered the best means of acceptance of a du'a. Indeed, Allaah commanded it when He said:

"To Allaah belong the Most Beautiful Names, so call upon Him by them."[43]

It is because of this that the majority of the du'a's narrated from the Prophet (peace and blessings of Allaah be upon him) and the prophets before him consist in seeking nearness to Allaah by way of His Names and His Attributes. As a result, the du'a would consist of what is appropriate from Allaah's Names and His Attributes, as it appears in the du'a of Allaah's Prophet, Shu'ayb (peace be upon him):

"Our Lord! Judge between us and our people in truth, for You are indeed the best of those who give judgment."[44]

And it has come in the du'a of Allaah's Messenger, Eesaa (peace be upon him):

"And provide for us, for You are the best of providers."[45]

And in the du'a, the Prophet (peace and blessings of Allaah be upon him) taught Abu Bakr (Allaah be pleased with him):

"O Allaah! Indeed, I have wronged myself a tremendous wrong-doing, and none forgives sins except You. So forgive me a forgiveness from You, and have mercy on me. Indeed, You are the Oft-Forgiving, the Most Merciful."[46]

The Prophet (peace and blessings of Allaah be upon him) even used to teach his ummah to seek nearness to Allaah by means of all His Most Beautiful Names. So he (peace and blessings of Allaah be upon him) said:

"No one suffers any sorrow or grief and he says: 'O Allaah! I am Your worshipper, the son of Your male worshipper, the son of Your female worshipper. My forelock is in Your hand, Your command over me is forever executed, and Your decree over me is just. I ask You by every name that belongs to You, by which You named Yourself, or revealed in Your Book, or taught to any of Your creation, or You have preserved in the knowledge of the unseen with you that you make the Qur'an the life of my heart and the light of my breast and a departure for my sorrow and a release for my anxiety." It was said, "O Messenger of Allaah! Shall we learn/memorize these words?" He said:

"Yes certainly. Whoever hears them should learn/memorize them."[47]

The statement of Imam Ibn al-Qayyim (Allaah have mercy on him), "and His Oneness" means that it is legislated and it is recommended to seek closeness to Allaah with this tremendous tool which is His Oneness and faith in Him. This is the greatest means of seeking nearness, rather it is the greatest and the loftiest of them.

From the conditions that support this type of seeking closeness is what Allaah mentioned from the du'a of the believers:

"Our Lord! Indeed, we have heard the call of one who calls to faith: 'Believe in your Lord', so we believed. Our Lord! Forgive us our sins and expiate from us our evil deeds, and cause us to die along with the righteous."[48]

When the Prophet (peace and blessings of Allaah be upon him) heard a man say:

"O Allaah! I beseech You indeed (by the fact that) I bear witness that You are Allaah, there is none worthy of worship but You, the One, the One to whom all objects turn to, the One who does not beget, nor was begotten, and there is nothing like You." Then he said (peace and blessings of Allaah be upon him):

"Indeed, you have asked Allaah by His Name, which He gives when He is asked by it, and when He is called by it, He answers."[49]

The Twelfth Condition

Giving charity before making du'a

Sadaqah (charity) is a tremendous affair. It has been authentically narrated that the Prophet (peace and blessings of Allaah be upon him) said:

"Charity in secret puts out the anger of Allaah."[50] There is no doubt that abating the wrath of ar-Rahman (the Most High) towards a worshiper is a reason for Him to answer his du'a and grant him that which he asked for. It is also among the common righteous acts which are legislated for the believer to use as a means of seeking nearness to Allaah.

The Thirteenth Condition

Striving to use the du'as which the Prophet (peace and blessings of Allaah be upon him) informed us of would be accepted

The Muslim, if he observes these narrated prayers (dua's) and he makes du'a with them with truthfulness, attention and earnestness along with the presence of all the previous matters, then his du'a would rarely be rejected.

An example of these prayers is the statement from the Prophet (peace and blessings of Allaah be upon him):

"The prayer of Dhun-Nun when he called and he was in the belly of the whale: 'There is nothing worthy of worship but You. Glorified are You. Indeed, I was one of the wrongdoers.' Indeed, no Muslim man makes du'a with it for anything except that Allaah will answer him."[51]

On the authority of Anas ibn Malik (Allaah be pleased with him) that the Prophet (peace and blessings of Allaah be upon him) heard a man say in his du'a:

"O Allaah! I ask of You because You are the One who is worthy of praise. There is nothing worthy of worship except You, the Ever-Generous, the Originator of the heavens and the earth. O One of Honor and Generosity! O Ever-Living! O Sustainer!" So the

Prophet (peace and blessings of Allaah be upon him) said:

"Indeed, He has called Allaah by His Greatest Name, which, if He is called by it, He answers, and if He is asked by it, He gives."

It has already been mentioned, the Dua of the man who sought closeness to Allaah with His Oneness and having faith in Him. So the Prophet (peace and blessings of Allaah be upon him) said:

"Indeed, you asked Allaah by the Name which if He is asked by it He gives, and if He is prayed to by it He answers."

Conclusion

So these are the general rules and ways of making du'a which were brought by al-Imam Ibn al-Qayyim (Allaah have mercy on him) so it is appropriate for every Muslim to strive to observe them in making du'a. Verily, whenever they are gathered, they are like what Ibn al-Qayyim (Allaah have mercy on him) mentioned: "This du'a, indeed, it is rare that it would be rejected."

We ask Allaah the Most High to rectify our religion for us, which is the protection of our affair, to rectify our worldly affairs, which contains our livelihood, and to rectify for us in our Hereafter, which is our final destination. We ask him to make living an increase for us in all good and dying a rest for us from all evil.

Allaah the Most High knows best. May Allaah bestow His praise, manifest His virtue and exalt the status of our Prophet Muhammad and protect him, the message of Islam, his family and all his companions from any harm in this life or the next.[53]

References

1

Surah al-Baqarah: 186

2

Surah al-A'raf: 55-56

3

=The Qur'an, for the Qur'an is a miracle and its recitation is worship and it is recited in Salah." Answered in Nur ' alad-Darb .

4

Reported by Muslim in his Saheeh, no. 2577.

5

Reported by at-Tirmidhee in Al-Jami', no. 3370. Al-Albanee rated it hasan in Saheeh al-Jami', no. 5392.

6

Reported by al-Tirmidhee in al-Jaami', No. 3373. Narrated by al -Albaani

Saheeh al-Jami', no. 2418.

7

Al-Jawab al- Kafee , p. 17.

8

9

Al-Jawab al- Kafee , pp. 16-17.

10

Reported by at-Tirmidhee in Al-Jami', no. 3479. Al -
Albanee rated it as hasan in As-Silsilah as - Saheehah,
no. 564.

11

Reported by Abu Nu'aym in Hilyat al-Awliya, 5/2

12

Saheeh al-Bukharee, no. 1145 and Saheeh Muslim, No.
758.

13

Reported by Abu Dawud in As-Sunan no. 524.
Narrated by al-Albaani in Saheeh Abee Dawud – Al-
Umm, no. 537.

14

Reported by Abu Dawud in his Sunan, no. 521, and at-Tirmidhee in his Jami', no. 212. Al -Albaani rated it saheeh in al- Irwa , no. 224.

15

Reported by at-Tayalasee in his Musnad, no. 524. Al-Albanee graded it saheeh in As-Silsilah as -Saheehah , no. 1413.

16

Reported by al-Bukharee in his Saheeh, no. 835, and by Muslim in his Saheeh, no. 402, and the wording is al -Bukharees .

17

Reported by al-Bukhari in his Saheeh, no. 6400, and by Muslim in his Saheeh, no. 852, and the wording is Muslim.

18

Reported by Muslim in his Saheeh, no. 853.

19

Reported by Muslim in his Saheeh, no. 482.

20

Reported by Abu Dawud in his Sunan, no. 1048. Al - Albaani graded it saheeh in Saheeh Abee Dawud – al-Umm

21

Zad -ul-Ma'ad, 1/377.

22

Surah al-A'raf: 55

23

Jami' al-Bayan fee Tafseer al- Qu'ran , 10/247.

24

Reported by al-Bukharee in his Saheeh, no. 2992, and Muslim in his Saheeh, no. 2704, and the wording is Muslim.

25

Fath- ul-Baree , 6/135.

26

Al-Minhaj Share Saheeh Muslim ibn al-Hajjaj, 17/25 .

27

Reported by Muslim in his Saheeh, no. 1763.

28

Reported by Abu Dawud in his Sunan, No. 17, and Ahmad in his Musnad, No. 1934, and the wording is Ahmad's. Al -Albanee rated it saheeh in As-Silsilah as - Saheehah , no. 834.

29

Reported by Abu Dawud in his Sunan, no. 1477. Al - Albaani graded it saheeh in Saheeh Abee Dawud – al-Umm, no. 1337.

30

Reported by Muslim in his Saheeh, no. 1763.

31

Reported by al-Bukharee in his Saheeh, no. 1030, and Muslim in his Saheeh, no.

895, and the wording belongs to Muslim.

32

Reported by Abu Dawud in his Sunan, no. 1481, and at-Tirmidhee in his Jami', no. 3477. Graded saheeh by al-Albaani, No. 1331.

33

See pages 14-16.

34

Reported by Muslim in his Saheeh, no. 1015.

35

Reported by al- Bayhaqee in Shu'ab al- Eeman , no. 1154.

36

Reported by Muslim in his Saheeh, no. 2702.

37

See Al-Jawab-ul- Kafee by Ibn al-Qayyim, p.15.

38

See As -Sihah Taj-ul- Loughah by al- Farabee , 4/1156 and Al -Qamus al -Muheet by al -Fayruz Abadee , p. 924.

39

Surah al-Anbiya: 90

40

Surah al-Mu'minun: 60

41

Surah al-Baqarah: 127

42

See Tafseer -ul-Qu'ran -il- 'Adheem by Ibn Katheer, 1/247.

43

Surah al-A'raf: 180

44

Surah al-A'raf: 89

45

Surah al-Ma'idah: 114

46

Reported by al-Bukharee in his Saheeh, no. 834, and Muslim in his Saheeh, no.

2705.

47

Reported by Imam Ahmad in his Musnad, no. 3712. Al- Albanee graded it saheeh in Al- Silsilah as-Saheehah , no. 199.

48

Surah Ali 'Imran: 193

49

Reported by Abu Dawud in his Sunan, no. 1493. Narrated by al-Albaani in Saheeh Abee Dawud – Al-Umm, no. 1341.

50

Reported by Al - Mu'jam al-Kabeer, no . 8014. Al - Albanee rated it saheeh in As - Silsilah as- Saheehah , no. 1908 by collecting its supporting narratives.

51

Reported by at-Tirmidhee in his Jami', no. 3505. Al - Albanee judged it saheeh in Takhreej al-Kalam at-Tayyib , no. 122.

52

Reported by Abu Dawud in his Sunan no 1495. Graded saheeh by al-Albaani in Sunan Bee Dawud – Al-Umm, no. 1342.

53

The origin of this thesis is a lecture I gave in the assembly of Ibraheem al - Wuqaysee in the city of the Prophet on Yawm al - Ithnayn (Monday) on the 24th day of Jumada al-Akhirah, 1441 H. Some of the students transcribed it and prepared it. I reviewed it, made corrections and added some benefits. We ask Allaah to reward all those who participated in producing this work, printing it and spreading it among the Muslims.

References:

1. The Du'a that is not rejected – Sh. 'Abdur-Razzaq al-Badr

2. Scholarly subtitles Youtube Video